THE LOST ROADS ADVENTURE CLUB

Also by R. M. Ryan

Goldilocks in Later Life

The Golden Rules

Vaudeville in the Dark

There's a Man with a Gun Over There

THE LOST ROADS ADVENTURE Club

POEMS

R. M. RYAN

LOUISIANA STATE UNIVERSITY PRESS
BATON ROUGE

Published by Louisiana State University Press
Copyright © 2017 by R. M. Ryan

All rights reserved
Manufactured in the United States of America
LSU Press Paperback Original
First printing

DESIGNER: Mandy McDonald Scallan
TYPEFACE: Whitman
PRINTER AND BINDER: LSI

Library of Congress Cataloging-in-Publication Data

Names: Ryan, R. M., author.
Title: The Lost Roads Adventure Club : poems / R. M. Ryan.
Description: Baton Rouge : Louisiana State University Press, [2017]
Identifiers: LCCN 2016027046 | ISBN 978-0-8071-6584-3 (pbk. : alk.
paper) | ISBN 978-0-8071-6585-0 (pdf) | ISBN 978-0-8071-6586-7 (epub) | ISBN
978-0-8071-6587-4 (mobi)
Classification: LCC PS3568.Y393 A6 2017 | DDC 811/.54—dc23
LC record available at https://lccn.loc.gov/2016027046

For my beloved teachers

Robert Dana
Jim Whitehead
John N. Morris
Howard Nemerov
George Hitchcock

Contents

PROLOGUE

Humpty Afterwards

You know
the story.

I was
broken

into
a million

little pieces,
a millionaire

of myself.
Of course

all the King's
horses

and
all the King's men

couldn't
put me

together again.
Get real.

Have you
ever seen

a horse
handle

a glue pot
or Knights,

with their
rusted

iron gloves,
assemble

the puzzle
of

a broken
egg?

Luckily
for me,

Jack—
or one

of those
other

fairy-tale
characters—

had
some

Elmer's
and—

voilà—

I got
glued

together
again.

Or almost.

Two pieces
of me

got
left out

in
the sunshine

and the rain.
Oh well.

So what
if my legs

stumble,
and I trip myself

occasionally.
So what?

Join me,
please,

as I trip
the light fantastic

into, yes,
the light.

PART I

On Angel Island, San Francisco Bay

That night camping
you showed me
the ship passing in the fog.

It seemed
to float there,
as if it were

sailing through a cloud
that perhaps includes
us as well, perhaps

fog is a just a cloud
anchored for a moment
here on earth,

on Angel Island,
much closer
to Heaven than we thought.

Along the Way This Morning

The air a dusk gray
as if we live
beneath a cloudy sea.

Lichen-covered rocks.
White mottling to black.
An old newspaper

slapped against one of them.
Perhaps the wind
was tired of the news.

The colored ads
for TV's, the face of Vanna White
from the *Wheel of Fortune*

turning into rock.
We're all breaking up.
I, for instance,

have carried
this smashed plum
on the bottom

of my fluorescent green
running shoes
from San Francisco to Vancouver,

bits of purpled plum skin
smeared like a wound
on the airport carpet

and now,
on the Vancouver sidewalk,
mixing with

the fallen magnolia blossoms:
confetti from a parade
that passed days ago.

I'm now passing as well,
along with the newspaper
crossword puzzle

flattened against the pavement
the word "glory" part gone,
almost looking like

"gore" in the stunning
glory of our defeat.

An Allegorical Everywhere

at the slots, Las Vegas

Hells Bells is the title of one machine.
Another is named for Michael Jackson.

Yet one more commemorates
the birth of the White Buffalo.

I wonder if people know this
occurred in Janesville, Wisconsin, in 1994.

Michael Jackson wanted to transform
himself into something else.

So here he is dancing forever
as long as the electricity lasts.

The white buffalo looks surprised
at where he's landed, maybe angry, too.

What's going on with us?
The stories never end. We get lost in them.

It's all one big allegory of everywhere.
Out in the desert, for instance, at Chaco Canyon,

the rocks look like giant human figures,
as large as the ones at Mount Rushmore.

Carved by accident? Maybe,
or maybe the Father of Days

left them for us to ponder,
the frowning god, the one who looks

down on us with some amusement.
But the joke is on him, too,

as the rain shales away
his Awesomeness into rubble.

It's all Ozymandias, baby.
Tutankhamun becoming Tweetie Bird.

Maybe it all gets recycled.
Here, at the slots in Vegas,

the music plays too loud.
"What Happened to My Heart?"

comes blaring, the chorus
repeating over and over again.

This would be a great place
for a nervous breakdown.

Michael Jackson looks surprised
at how his wishes have come true.

Electric immortality.
I hope this isn't heaven.

Maybe the White Buffalo wants to talk
some sense into us

as we make our way
through the labyrinth of all our days.

Hotel Nevada

That hit the note, didn't it? Coming fast
Into Gabbs on 391,
The big BMW cycle doing—
What?—80? 5,000 RPM,

The Dvořák String Trio on my headphones,
That run of notes which always breaks my heart,
Just below the mine arrayed like a hotel
On the mountain, the lady in the general store

Lit by a fluorescent bulb almost flickered out
Was uncertain about what they did there.
"I think they're mining something that begins
With *P*," she said and circled her cigarette

As if it might all be smoke. "You want
The other lights on?" For what? I wondered.
The Produce Department was 3 sizes of potatoes.
"No, thanks," I said and rode the gravel road

Toward the park with the Ichthyosaur fossil.
Man, that baby wasn't smoke at all
Out there behind another mine—this one hot
For gold and silver in 1908, two hundred

People here—including a prostitute
And an undertaker—to get the million bucks
The earth was holding like a bank deposit,
But the Ichthyosaur lay 200 million

Years before anyone thought to take
Her out. They mined her, too, starting
With—what else?—dynamite. Jackhammers
Next—backhoes, Caterpillar tractors—

"The whole American shebang to get us to
This level," the guide told our three-man tour
Standing under the A-frame that protects
The Ichthyosaur as if she's retired to

A cozy Triassic suburb after all
The terrible tons of time left her wide-
Eyed and open mouthed, her scattered bones
Squirted through with veins of liquid crystal.

I tried to figure it out later that night,
In the casino of the Hotel Nevada, playing
Texas Hold 'Em, looking for a queen
To match my little pair. When I got her,

I slid 40 bucks out to bet. "You're getting
In over your head," the man next to me added
As he matched my bet. Aren't we all? I thought,
Beneath these tufts of clouds that don't yet

Add up to water, to floods and cataclysms—
You know—the big-bang stuff of centuries
When the earth takes back our little bets.
I lost my 40 bucks to his full house

And later walked outside in the night air.
Two drunks got into their Dodge Ram
2500 V10. Straight pipes
Out the back; the starry night ahead;

The full moon and its mournful, shot-up face.
"Just listen," the driver said, spewing gravel
All over the parking lot. "Just listen
To the way this baby fires when you hit the gas!"

Prayer Teeth

A miniature white-washed church,
A ten-foot tall bell tower,
An arched doorway so low you had to stoop
Your way in, a bench for three, an altar
Braided with dried flower petals, the window
Cracked all over but held together somehow—
Shivers from a long-ago ecstasy.

"You see these everywhere in Greece,"
Mr. Constantine said, "dedicated
To Saint Someone's apparition here—
Little lonely altars on the roads."

This one, though, was different: it was manned
By a hunchbacked priest (or maybe just
A crazy man in robes) who welcomed us,
Speaking a toothless kind of Latin-Greek
Mr. Constantine had trouble understanding.

All of us crowded inside, and the priest chanted
And prayed and then held up a rusted metal
Coffee can. "*Pacem Deus Irae.*"
Peace to the angry God, he seemed to say
And pulled out of the can, on a golden chain,
A rosary of teeth. "I think they're his,"
Mr. Constantine whispered. The old hunchback
Held them up, chanting as he fingered them.
"Prayer teeth," I think he said.

This all came back to me
The night Gloria Emmerling drove
Her Chrysler Pacifica into the sea.
Suicide or accident? Who knows?
The car did backflips down the cliff,
Scattering stuff we found for days, including
This lanyard that must have hung from her rear-view mirror
With a Dream-Catcher, the Queen of Spades, and a little glass
Hole-drilled heart. What dreams
Were caught there, I don't know. Mine
Now I guess—Mr. Constantine and me,
The toothless priest counting his troubles out.
Pacem Deus Irae. Praying for the best.
A few last teeth for the altars up ahead.

Along the Road to Drama

Macedonia

Now that The Man
with the Blue Guitar

plays in Chicago
and is turning red

as if embarrassed
by how things have gone,

everything has changed
and you get to thinking

how art isn't much longer
than life anymore.

What's happened to
those stern pillars

in the hard sun?
How about the mist, the gods

hidden but about
to emerge at the Crack

of Dawn and the oracles
down from the mountaintops

with those heavy hexameters?
Oh the gypsies have started

a little parade with these tootings
on the zurna and the beat

of the daouli and we're dancing again
along the road to Drama

and I'll take your hand
if you hold on to mine.

Here in Paradise

We're living here
in Paradise, California,

in this rundown
rented house.

What we thought
we knew

in the green delight
of the afternoon

has yellowed
like a 60's photograph.

What we did for laughs
is not so funny anymore

in the light that lingers.
Oh look how it's all

just the finger
you pointed at the moon.

that night we stood
lost in starlight on the lawn,

me in my old blue jeans
you in that ragged blouse

living out our days
in that rundown rented house.

wondering whose directions
got us lost

unable to pay the cost
of renting all our days

as the years roll by
and the stars spin round.

Let's you and me be long gone
with our dancing shoes on

here in Paradise
in a rundown rented house.

Someone's Essential Wisdom

What was the name
of that church in Lima?

Right downtown.
Ancient. A hulking fortress

leaning from earthquake damage.
Our little tour group,

maybe ten of us,
climbing the narrow stair

to the choir loft.
On my right

as we came to the top
was an ancient library

with huge leather-bound
books. Pages of dusty vellum

all white—or really
gray with age,

someone's essential wisdom
about the mysteries of the world,

must-reads then,
forgotten now.

To my left a balcony
that looked down upon

a meager congregation.
Then the woman beside me

said "Oh my God,"
and started to sob,

and I saw just what she meant.
Shafts of light

from high-up windows
fell on the heads of a few,

as if these
were The Awakened Ones

singing in their cracked voices
of the redemption from the earth.

The light fell on us, too,
and who really cared

what the church
was called?

It could've been
St. Anyone

as the hidden organ
played the lifting chords:

St. Her or Him or Me
and even, yes, St. You.

Waimanalo Beach

How tender
the way the sunrise

turns gray clouds
into gold.

The little purple shovel
a child has forgotten on the sand

goes out with waves
and comes back in again

as if trying
to make up its mind.

The turtle—
God bless the turtle—

struggles up the beach,
leaving the fierce pull

of the ocean behind,
blinking, looking at me

surprised that the two of us
are together here at last.

Youth

Remember?
It was down Milwaukee Avenue

then left on Main
if we went the short way

or all the way to the Five Points
and then up Court

if we went the long way.
Then it was left on Atwood

and back down Milwaukee.
We did this for hours

when I was seventeen.
Round and around

dreaming of where we'd go
when we got out of Janesville—

down Milwaukee, back up Court
round and around, and around once more.

The Adrian X-Ray Shoe Fitter

I recall snowy nights
when the world

seemed
to shut down

at 4:30
in the afternoon,

as if someone
had pulled

the shades:
a sky dirty

as old cotton balls
that hid

something hard
in Janesville

where we boys
waited

for our transfer
buses

at the Corn Exchange,
the snow-dusted monument

to past commerce.
Bored,

we'd throw snowballs
at each other,

getting little pieces
of that dirty

sky on our faces.
When the bus

was late
we'd wander—

one by one—
into the shoe store

whose name
I've forgotten,

past the illuminated
plastic goose

to the Adrian
X-Ray Shoe Fitter

and watch the bones
of our feet wiggle

until we got the giggles
and ran back

to throw more snowballs.
I got out of Janesville,

but many of boys
throwing snowballs

that late afternoon
didn't. No,

they went on
to work

at the Chevrolet Plant
or the Parker Pen Company,

where they made pens
for the people like me

to write with.
They worked

until the plants closed
leaving them out of work,

some drunk, some dead.
We had no idea then

of how dangerous
the comic Adrian

could be,
throwing radiation

around the room.
nor did we realize

that the cloud-dirty
sky held messages

saying "Get out of town
before it's too late,"

before the Universal
Dark comes down around you.

PART II

The Lost Roads Adventure Club

The gods
paint over things
as if they

are still trying
to get the look
of the earth just right.

The woman
in her Roman garden,
80 years old,

staring at
the sunburnt roses
and the yellow earth.

"In all my years
I have never seen
anything like it."

The mushroom
cloud out over the Pacific
in 1953

like an *i*
with a fat dot,
though somehow and

impossibly the world goes on:
the roses
or others like them

are restored to bloom.
It's all
killing us

but others keep coming
to replace us.
I think of this

as I drive along,
killing things myself
with my car.

Bright butterflies
are smeared on my windshield
like abstract paintings.

The Neverlost ® option
on my rent-a-car
is stuck on directions

for some other city,
and the droning mechanical
voice directs me to nowhere

as I follow the directions
in my head, though finally
it gives up.

"If possible," the voice says,
"make a U-turn."
Go back, go back:

to where, though?
Where Death waits
to smear me

like a blurred Cezanne
on someone's windshield?
No.

In this,
The Lost Roads Adventure Club,
I'm going

where I ought to go:
toward a new world
while the old one dies.

Good Night, Irene

The Weavers' version of "Goodnight, Irene"—
my family, sitting around the dining table,

singing off key—me sixteen,
my head on the table, so fucking embarrassed,

just able to see the TV in the other room—
Goodnight, Irene, I'll see you in my dreams.

Oh, I wanted out of there,
wanted to live on the other side of that TV screen

where I couldn't hear them,
where I'd own those perfect goods.

That would take care of me.
Gone my father's bad tenor

and the strange bass notes of the women underneath—
the six of them singing their way through

"Goodnight Irene." I, I, I—
me, I'm rising up, ("Where are you going?"

"Just out with Brian"), so embarrassed by it all.
Goodnight, Irene, they're all dead, buried

in ten square feet (I measured it one winter afternoon)
there at Oak Hill Cemetery, and me—I'm out

of there, lifted to the level I wanted so badly
to find, Irene, I'll see you in my dreams,

rearranging my goods, counting on them,
their cracked voices clearer and clearer.

A Memory

I was driving across the desert
in 100 degree heat.

The mountains
shimmered

like the bottoms
of seas.

For some reason
I thought

of a lady
I once knew

and how tightly
she was wound up

and how
we ended up

in bed
and how I began

kissing
her feet

and then
moved on,

both of us
shaken loose,

and I thought
of that

driving
across the desert,

watching the play
of light

where mystic
illusions of purple seas

came and went
and came again.

Save the Last Dance for Me

to the sweet memory of Doc Pomus and Mort Shuman

Betty Tiegs is in my arms,
her head on my shoulder,

her body coiled into a tight
question mark against me.

That's White Shoulders perfume
she's wearing, and my head fills with the scent

of Miss Hunuska, the sexiest woman I know.
She sat beside me in fourth-grade music class.

I strummed, and she played the push keys
of that autoharp, and I'm stroking

the allowed part
of Betty Tiegs's back

between her bra strap and the top of her panties,
though once in a while I touch a forbidden place

lightly and she nestles even closer
and I have the beginnings of a hard-on

and it's The Drifters, oh, The Drifters
Save the Last Dance for Me

The Drifters, oh, the Drifters
Under the Boardwalk, Up on the Roof

everywhere, and everywhere, The Drifters
as we try to hold the world around us

ever more tightly
in our arms.

My Villanelle

I lost my villanelle.
Where it went,
no one could tell.

I looked high
and then . . . well, you can tell . . .
I looked in that other place as well,

searching for my villanelle
but no one could tell
what happened to my villanelle.

I miss my little villanelle.
It kept me company
when I sat a spell

contemplating
the moments as they fell
down the waterfall of my villanelle—

the crystal drops of water
as they fell
sparkling in the sunshine of my villanelle

into the quiet pond
past the shady reaches of the well,
into the pond The Ancients called *It All Ends Well*,
here at the ending of my villanelle.

Embraced in Light

Remember the annoying street peddler in Oaxaca
pestering us to buy the little carved knickknack?

He wouldn't leave us alone that afternoon on the Zócalo,
but it was all so sweet, wasn't it?

A little breeze in the linden trees,
and the sun delicious: just-right, soft and warm

like the heated-up pastry I bought.
Remember the guys in the marimba band

and the school girls in their matching dresses
twirling as they walked, their skirts lifting up

as if they might rise to heaven all by themselves?
Everyone seemed so happy

I thought, and maybe that's when
my cancer began to go away.

That's about when the guy came up with this
painted wooden ornament like an amulet—

a crescent moon embracing the sun.
It made a kind of sense, really,

seeing them holding each other close like that—
lovers, though the actual sky is full of separation

so much darkness between the stars
and I think of all the lost souls fallen

at Thermopylae and Stalingrad
and places no one's heard of

like the Battle of Changping (700,000 dead)
or the Brusilov Offensive (1,600,000 lost there),

names that broke all those families' hearts
while History forgot them

like a man with dementia
stumbling on to fight some more.

Thank God for the Zócalo just then:
you and I there, the girls twirling,

the salsa tune like sunlight bouncing off the marimba
and the little wooden ornament

with the moon and the sun lovers now
haloed by a little ring of smiling skulls

meaning, I guess, that the dead
wish the best for each and every one of us

as they circle round that unity of light.
Of course we'd all smile if we were doing that—

putting the world back together again as if
Humpty Dumpty never fell.

No more battles, ever, to fight,
in a universe with so much to see and smile about:

the Zócalo, lovers like us, the peddler who made the sale:
the sun and moon embraced in so much light.

A Little Poem For Jennifer, 1952–2009

All the stories
Never told:
Petals fallen
From the rose.

What Science Shows Us

Tears from laughter,
tears from change.

Tears from onions,
tears from grief.

All different
beneath the microscope.

Crystals arranged
like cities, shorelines, and flakes of snow.

The snowflakes
freeze the onions out.

Laughter is a mess
going everywhere all at once.

Change is a city
moving into a forest,

or a forest
moving into a city.

And grief, oh, grief
is trying to connect

Tears from laughter,
tears from change.

Tears from onions,
tears from grief.

The Immeasurable Sunshine

Vas bien.

1.
I was happy, actually—
Ecstatic if you want to know the truth—

When I found out
That all the knots of worry

I had tied so carefully
And stored there

In the upper right corner of my back—
All the terrible weight

Of the world
I'd lifted every single day—

All of that,
Like the money

I obsessively saved . . .
All of it made, at last, perfect sense.

A nice 3 cm rectangle growing . . .
Cancer, ah yes,

Becoming the immortality
I so badly wanted—

All I couldn't let go of
Banked like my money—

Yes, I thought,
Delirious with the thought—

I'd done it
And I remembered

My father's cancer
In exactly the same place.

Yes, a family tradition
Of death.

"You see, you," he . . .
Now *I* was saying . . .

That's where I hurt all along.
That's why I drank,

Why I smoked those cigarettes,
Drank those fourteen cups of tea each day . . .

I meant to sooth that self-inflicted pain,
To smooth it out.

And now I had it,
All my history—

Wars, financial collapse—
All the bad stuff I worried about,

Praying "Oh, God, no
Not me, not your special one,

Not me, no,"
But meaning exactly that,

Longing really
To meet my family

Where they waited
In that ten square feet

Of Heaven's Parlor,
Out there in Oak Hill Cemetery.

My father brother mother
Aunt uncle grandfather grandmother

And—at last—me,
For the final symmetry

Of my few feet there:
A little park

4 feet by 8
Named just for me.

2.
Are you kidding?
I'm not doing that!

I'm going to beat this thing—
This hardheaded little 3 cm

Tiny bully I had trained to kill me.
What is that

Against
The immeasurable sunshine?

3.
I am riding now
In Antonio's Lada

On Avenida de los Presidentes
in Centro Habana.

It's a sort of a taxi
With a hand-carved wooden dash

And salsa blaring from the radio.
"Histórica real," the announcer says.

Does that mean real history,
Or the history declared by kings?

Then, who finally cares?
As we drive along, filling the air

With fumes from the ancient engine,
The brakes screeching, the steering

Just a memory
As we go through red lights

On the edge of death.
But how is this different

From the man forewarned—
Running from Death

Only to find Death waiting
In the closet of the room where the man hid?

Antonio and me
We don't care.

Nah.
We're driving along,

Singing at the top of our lungs,
Our own words

To someone else's song,
Honking.

Our friends,
On the edge of their own death,

Honking back,
Waving at us,

At the DeSotos and the Nash Ramblers
And the other ancient cars

At the sky
And whatever

The sky brings us
From the East.

Song at the End of This

I want to live
where the bougainvillea blooms.
I want to think
where my thoughts have rooms.

Poems, a story or two,
some paintings on the wall,
Beethoven blasting through my head—
and a place to hear the Muses call.

A town to walk
where petals carpet things—
pink rugs on my way home
and purple when I sing.

PART III

How to Get There

Coming the wrong way out of Palmyra,
heading west instead of east

around that curve on 59,
the fields laid out like closed books

in brown and darker brown and black,
this late November day,

the feathery tree limbs a burnt haze
now that their leaves are lost

in the iron light of evening—
coming the wrong way

toward this sign
Lessons Available—Just Ahead.

A Triplet

That was then,
and this is now,

though that's gone, too,
I don't know how.

Figuring that out
will take a lot more *now*'s.

About the Light

In the bleached light
of afternoon,
we're just
a disappearing act.

So much has faded,
though is this
something to be frightened of?

Why be afraid
of going where
the light has gone?

.

Meditation

O how long
Until

Every thought's
A poem.

We thought
We were lost

When, really,
We were on our way home.

Parasailor Out over the Ocean

Held up
by color
and the wind,

the center
of the universe
keeps moving

to and fro
as the waves below
come rolling in.

Shhh, shhh
they seem to say.
It all goes spinning round

no matter what we do.
Sweet Baby,
be at peace

as you go nowhere
and everywhere all at once
embraced by color and the wind.

A Furious Energy

Two hawks,
yes,

diving
and swooping,

with each other.
Then one rides

the other's back,
a furious energy,

upside down,
right side up,

impossible
to follow,

making the mark
of infinity.

6:30 A.M. This Morning

The moon lingers
as if
it doesn't want to go.

Ah, that life
goes by
but life goes slow.

At the Lost-Roads Institute

It's all *perhaps*
in the curriculum here—
along with staring out the window,
long pauses, and lots of naps.

Fall Leaves

Golden once,
Now just brown,

The oak leaves learn
The one way out of town.

Hide-and-Seek

Notes
And the echoes
Of notes.

What I thought
And what
I wrote.

Similar
But not
The same.

The hide-and-seek
Of meaning
And its name.

This Evening

In Trastevere,
In the twilight,
I sit here,
Trying to write.

Tap, tap, click,
Tap, tap, click

In Trastevere,
In the twilight
While the day
Goes wheeling overhead,
I sit here
Among the living and the dead

In Trastevere,
In the twilight

Trying to say something
About the alleyway
Where the sun is going
Fast oh fast
And nothing brilliant's
Meant to last

In Trastevere,
In the twilight

Tap, tap, click
I conclude.
Tap, tap, click.

Then: *All the Best,*
Your Servant,

Rick

Keatsian

No one ever mentions
The wear and tear:
A thing of beauty
Needs constant repair

The Sandpiper

Look at him go,
this fluff of nothing

back and forth along the shore,
avoiding the waves,

beaking his way along
as if adding periods

to unseen sentences—
or maybe to sentences

he can see
but we cannot.

Who knows
as we, ourselves, go,

two fluffs of nothing,
you and I,

avoiding the waves,
back and forth along the shore.

The Farm I Bought

The black cattle in the stubble field.
The snow swirling.

They seem content
as suddenly

so do I
beneath

the huge acres
of the gray sky

all of us
in the lovely

stunning world
walking beside each other

on the way
to the killing floor.

Hold Me

Do we mean
What we say
On the Prado?

In Cienfuegos,
The kindergarten girl
With her Princess backpack,

Her mother
In the skin-tight t-shirt
Super Sexy Hold Me.

The woman going by
Kiss, Kiss it says
Across her breasts.

Just so, but then
We have to include
The policemen

With their pistols
And another view of things.
The bang, bang, baby

Of the turning world
The Little Princess dead,
Super sexy lost forever.

Bang, bang, baby, bang bang.
Just so. Let's pray
To put the guns away,

Hold me, Darling One
Hold Me, Hold Me, please
As the spinning world goes round

Faster than we might believe,
We're on our knees
Hold me, hold me, please.

Wallace Stevens

What the lovely
baubles

of the world
reveal

as they lie
shattered

on the ground
is nothing

so well
as light,

pure light,
reflecting

back
on us.

Me, I'm Headed for the Carnival

The sword swallower
never comes around anymore.

The Fat Lady's
eating White Castles

at the hockey game.
She takes them from a bag

like potato chips.
No wonder

The Freak Show
died.

It's all around us now:
Dillinger's Escape Car,

now a Minivan,
sits riddled with bullet holes

in a border-town
vacant lot.

Vaya con Dios, baby,
though you've got to wonder:

have I taken up
with the wrong God?

Who's gonna
straighten out

the mess?
Whole Foods perhaps

with its eight types
of garbage,

and I stand there
wondering what to do

the way I did
on those IQ tests

when all the answers
looked correct to me.

Look: here's
my bag of garbage.

You turn it in
for me.

Me, I'm headed for
the Carnival

We're setting up
our show, unfurling

those cracked banners
before the soldiers,

in their creased pants, arrive.
Step right up

into The Funhouse Mirror
and see that you're

The Fat Lady now.
You just need

a few tattoos.
Take Fortune's Ride

and see if you ever come back
to where the soldiers,

with their safeties off,
wait patiently.

Dvořák

Were his fingers fat?
That's how I imagine them,

Imagine, too, a fine
Filigree of sweat across his brow

As he walks the meadows
Around Spillville, Iowa,

The tower of St. Wenceslas Church
Hidden behind that elm on this

Fine morning, with mist rising,
As if the earth were breathing,

Birds scattering in the air
Like notes

On the invisible
Score of the sky.

Dvořák humming,
The butcher's boy,

A butcher himself actually,
Trained in that

In case the music
Didn't work out.

He hums a tune from Bach,
The bells of All Saints calling across the meadow,

The birds do rearrangements
In the air, and Dvořák

Whistles, his body rocking
With the melody he's plucked

From where he sits
In the shade below the elm,

His fat fingers opening up the pen,
Writing the melody on his shirt cuff.

He's got it, then,
For us—the sky, the day, the birds,

The cows grazing on the farther hills,
The soon-to-be-disappearing elm.

The Christmas Pageant

We are wise
only if we play our parts
and build a Bethlehem
inside our hearts.

PART IV

"I Can't Get Over the Sunsets Here"

—on the coast of California

These sunsets received an Honorable Mention in
a newspaper readers' poll. Pleasant, eh?—
ambling through the evening's showered light
pouring like a waterfall on everything.
Easy to believe that the world is kind and means us well.

What, then, is this other stuff?—feathers
scattered here, as if a bird exploded.
Was it Emily Dickinson's "thing with feathers"—hope,
the flutter in the chest—which bit the dust?
And what is the awful smell? The beached whale

on the pristine beach, its back a row of shark bites
like a partly open zipper. Last month,
it was a poor dead harbor seal, his eyes
plucked out, turkey vultures helping him
off with his coat in nature's restaurant.

Aye, Lads, the brutal has its beauties, too—
the appropriate red of the turkey vulture's head,
the way they urinate on their yellow talons
to clear the rotten carrion away.
Was it you that wanted men to match these mountains?

Fat chance, Buddy. In nature's Super Bowl,
it isn't the Cowboys versus the Steelers in some
beer-commercialed allegory of America.
This is the slow grind promised by the schoolroom clock.
The slow grind of the mountains into silt,

and the way the ocean laps away the coast.
Mud is our manifest destiny.
I love those radio dish antennae, like hands
cupped over our ears, listening to
the static of outer space, as if hoping

for instructions on a way out of here.
If you ask me, that static sounds like sand,
especially on the days when I feel just the slightest
slippage underneath my feet and briefly
have this vision that I'm skiing down

some hidden hill of sand. "Oh look,
Honey," a mother says, pointing out
the feathers on the path. "This means
an angel landed here." We could go with her on this,
but I've come to like the little *frisson* of fear

chasing that fluttering bird of mine around
its cage. I love these cracked and towering rocks
splintered from the terrible tons of time. *Ker-blowie's*
the word for this, Action Comics as good
a guide as Kierkegaard, so yes, let's

have it all, please, angels and action
figures, Emily Dickinson, too,
and sit here, figuring nothing out, as we watch
the way the sky seems flushed with fire,
the continent behind us all the way on this.

1020 Putnam Avenue

In the town where I grew up
At 1020 Putnam Avenue—
In the rooming house
My mother ran
Where factory workers like Eddie Forslund lived
With my family—
One yearly ritual of the men
Was the opening of trout season in the spring.

In 1952, I was seven.
Eddie helped me, but I had
My own rod and reel, my own tin of salmon eggs.
I was out there at 5 a.m. by the bridge
Below the power plant—
Maybe thirty men and boys were there
Walking in the mud beside the river,
Mud sucking off my shoes.
I was one of the guys,
And my fingers were bloody from trying
To bait my hook with salmon eggs in the dark.

Much later, after my shift at Fairbanks Morse
Was done and I sat at the Hilltopper Tap
Nursing my Seven-Seven in the purple light
Of the bar that made
Ordinary paper fluorescent as if
Our bruised lives were meant for other things—
The back-bar beckoned like success.
Johnny Walker, Crown Royal, Korbel—
What I'd drink when I got rich. . . .

Eddie Forslund yells "Over here!"
As, barefoot, I keep falling in the mud,
Fish nowhere to be seen,
Wondering what I'm fishing for.

Later, in the fall, another season of the men:
Deer this time—
Dead and bloody bucks
Slumped across Chevy fenders.

That was the car they built in my hometown,
And I worked at the Chevy factory one summer.
That was the time I caught fire
From the exploding naphtha fumes
Of the fluid we used
To make sure the cars were clean
Before they got painted.

It was the Army after that,
Hoping the bullets
Were meant for someone else,
And then the 2 percent raises and the place up north

And still I hear him in the dark—
Eddie, I think. Eddie Forslund in the dark,
Amid the shadowy movements of the men—
Is that you Eddie, still out there,
Making payments on your brand-new '52,
Is that you yelling, while I try to find my shoes,
You yelling
"It's over here, right over here"?

The Stuff I Figured Out

Ein Heldenleben, you bet,
Though this morning the Strauss sounds—
Oh, I don't know—a little weary,
All that chasing around after enemies

That change their costumes every year,
Sometimes against you, sometimes your friend.
I think of those poor knights at the end
Of Chivalry, unhorsed by some bobo

With sticks. Those poor knights
Lying there. . . . if left long enough,
Their hinges must have rusted shut.
They couldn't go all that far from home

Or go anywhere without a can of oil.
Why, this morning, those knights
Remind me of the year I got
A microscope for Christmas

When I was ten as if my parents thought
I was going to be a scientist someday.
I sat up in my room making these little slides
Of stuff and studying them and taking notes

Just the way *The Junior Guide to Science*
Said to do in my *Junior Guide to Scientific Observation*.
All I found out, alas,
Was that what I didn't know

Got closer in and bigger—sometimes
With ridges and colors I couldn't see
With the naked eye. If I were one
Of those important guys, I'd give

What I didn't know a Latin name
And go on a slide-show lecture tour.
Maybe this little rock which resists us
Knowing anything about it

Has been the Philosopher's Stone all along,
Making what I'll never know much heavier
Than my lightweight catalog of *The Stuff I Figured Out*.
The old *Heldenleben*, yes—

The Don Quixote thing: tilting at—
Well, not windmills. We got rid of those,
And, oh, I think he fell down centuries ago,
Remember?—and we left him there

Until he rusted shut.
It's Sancho Panza now
In a backward baseball cap and wooden stick
Slashing through the air

The way he thought his master did,
Thinking he'll get somewhere.
He reminds me of my optimistic dog
Wagging her tail

Suddenly enthusiastic
For the same old stale room
That bored her to death
Fifteen minutes ago.

Still what fun
To bend over the microscope,
Bringing the Unknown
Into perfect focus,

Writing it down
Giving it a name
Just as if we know
Exactly what we're talking about.

Memories Are Made of This

for Dean Martin

That RCA in the sunroom,
me in front of it—I could have been the dog
in those long-ago ads, my ear cocked,

playing over and over the two 45's I owned.
"Blueberry Hill" and "Memories Are Made of This."
I'm singing along, hitting some of the notes,

as loud as I can, "I found my thrill." Yes.
"It lingered until." The '57 Ford
is passing by in slow motion. "That's

the car to have," Ollie Webb tells us boys
and Mrs. Schooley nods as she sweeps the sidewalk
and Mr. Hammerlund bends over to pick up

his *Rockford Morning Star*, and Quinn Boyle's
father has a Grundig radio he
brought home after the War from Germany

and he tells us we can tune in the far away
on its short-wave dial, but all we hear is static
while overhead the satellites circle as if

we're all the center of something, but then—then—
Elvis is in the Army and something's different
about the world and more and more satellites

are above us and the '57's have gone
about their business somewhere else
and Mrs. Schooley's splayed on the sidewalk

beside her broom as if she fell from the sky.
A stroke, my mother says and my dad is dying
and we're surrounded at Khe Sanh, the .45's

firing in the dark and the security system
in my suburban house says "Perimeter Armed"
and we know it's really not and wonder if

the *beep, beep, beep* of those satellites
meant nothing more than *beep, beep, beep.*
At the end of the 45's the needle goes

click, click, click amplified
in the sunroom on East Memorial Drive
and here, as I write this in the little café,

some sunlight left to go this afternoon,
the old drunk has found a few brown-spotted
bouquets to sell. Flowers for last year's

birthdays, but flowers nonetheless,
and still Dino's singing from the box
Sweet, sweet, the memories you gave to me.

At a Distance of My Own

How is it—
returning from the house in the woods
on the bread-crumb trail, holding my sister's hand—

that we got separated and no matter how hard
we yelled and stamped our feet
and yelled *Here I am*,

we got farther and farther apart.
I sat there crying
at the uselessness of it all

until I actually started feeling better,
and I remembered stories of boys
raised by animals in the wilderness

and saw, then, looking at me,
birds, just out of reach,
but studying me as I studied them,

so I followed along at a distance of my own
especially the pair of cardinals
who hopped from tree to tree,

the male like a bloody heart through the air,
the female you didn't notice right away
but a brown luminescence afterwards.

Where now was the boy
raised by the wilderness, I wondered
as I came out of the woods behind the birds.

I was now the company of crows
who loudly celebrated something,
and a white egret like a pale exclamation point

throwing something over and over in the air
rubbery like a ball.
My God, those balls were frogs!

She was eating frogs, throwing them in the air
and swallowing them as they fell:
all those potential princes gone.

Where now was the boy
raised by the wolves I wondered
as I walked on up the road—

not toward home but toward somewhere else.
There were other cries in the distance now of *Here I am.*
The crows, still in their loud party,

walked stiffly, rocking from side to side,
sometimes hopping just ahead of me
as if they knew the way

to wherever it was
the boy raised by the wilderness
had gone.

The Night Shift,
Fairbanks Morse, 1965

for Gene Amyotte

It was Bruno, Mr. Ed, and me
showing our badges and safety glasses

to the guard, who waved us through
the turnstile bars of the Engine Plant,

where once they made the giant diesels
that powered destroyers, aircraft carriers,

and submarines but that War—the Big War,
that War, Bruno said—was long over,

"Done, finito, toodle-oo, goodbye,"
and now the same engines generated power

for satellite-tracking stations as if
we were taking the war into the heavens.

My first job was chiseling
dried varnish from the inside

of an enormous steel vat.
I sat in its bottom every night

for eight hours with two ten-minute breaks
and a half hour for lunch.

"You're starting at the bottom,"
Mr. Ed told me. "Nowhere to go

but up." Oh he laughed at that
and called me a Corporate Executive

when we ate our lunches at four
in the morning, sitting there

in the doorway to the dark.
Later I was promoted to coil winder,

and stood beneath a three-story
Palladian window in that old factory

winding yard after yard
of cloth-covered copper wire into patterns

intricate as a weaving for the gods
while the moon arced across the sky.

Then they made me the driver
of a forklift truck, and I roamed

the acres of that huge factory,
moving giant engine parts

for one machinist to another.
I carried pistons the size of men

in the two arms of that fork lift
as if I were bringing in the wounded.

It's 1965. Our enemies
are all around us, Bruno says,

coming through the perimeter in the dark.
Bruno's a religious man and would stand,

at the beginning of our lunch break,
holding his Stanley Thermos up

toward the night sky. "Lord," he'd say,
"I offer myself to you . . ."

"Bullshit," said Mr. Ed. Me, I sat there
wondering where any of this was going.

It was 1965. Our enemies are out there,
circling us, firing in the dark.

"The world's a dangerous place," Bruno says,
shaking the last drops from Stanley Thermos

into his mouth, and we look around
in the 4 a.m. night. I'm a shiver of nerves,

and the days go by, and pretty soon
it's 1969, and my number's up

and I'm summoned to the War,
but I survive and the days still go by

faster and faster, and Fairbanks Morse
is broke, and the Palladian window

is covered up, and I wonder what
my coils are tracking in the obsidian night,

and I learn that our enemies never existed.
They were just shadows in the dark

and I am carrying this giant piston
for some lost motor. I carry it

toward the night like an offering.
It is 1965, in the middle of the night.

The River

It's low,
its mouth stalled
as if it had
nothing to say,
the water backing up—
brown, foamy slime
gathering there,
and the steelhead
who made it back
after being gone for years,
after traveling thousands of miles
from black pool to black pool
to make their way
up the final hundred miles
to spawn and die—
the steelhead . . .
why the steelhead are trapped
in the shallow water.

And the fishermen!
More fishermen than I've ever seen
out there on the river
where they seem to walk
a sparkling road of water
into the late afternoon sun
scooping up the fish
into their nets,
the fish too tired to fight
and the osprey,
cruising overhead,
suddenly drops,
out of nowhere, a fish
in his talons
like a sign of what

can happen to all of us.
Then the two of them rise up,
impossible seeming,
the bird and the fish overhead
up a hundred, two hundred,
then hundreds of feet in the air,
into the sere air,
which must burn the gills
of the fish the way
ice-cold water
would sting our lungs,
the fish overhead,
its red-hot belly
full of sex and spawn
soaring above the river
and maybe it's here
in the terror of its dying
when time slows to nothing—
an eternity before
the lights go out—
the fish has this vision
such clarity after
the shifting shadows
beneath the water
in the ecstatic terror

and I'm watching this
in my clumsy body
with eyes that have looked
for sixty-eight years
at the world for meaning
and maybe this,
this right here
is another lifetime

for the fish, the osprey, and me
a kind of heaven
on the river
for all of us
wherever—
heavy,
and longing for
the lightness of the air.

Amazing Stories

We devoured them, didn't we?
On those afternoons, our heads
Propped up as we sprawled across the floor.

What was it when we started out?
The Hardy Boys chasing U-Boats
With their father's Chris Craft Runabout.

Had we the chance, we'd do all that
—And more! The Tell-Tale Heart was ours of course,
Trapped inside the walls of our little lives.

We'd be brilliant, wouldn't we? Capturing
The Rue Morgue murderer
And then taking off on the rocket ship

To Verna. Remember how it was hidden in the silo?
Or there on Ratüfel's Expedition to darkest Africa,
One leg broken, an eye-patch on, staggering

Into Truhardt's Camp just in time to see
The fur-bound book. How sticky it was to turn
Its pages and feel them take us in.

Ah, the damask curtains, the sunset ocean view.
We put our hearts into it, you and I.
It isn't just Keats whose living hand is trapped

On a page somewhere. No, it's whole libraries of us,
Our restless hands turned entirely to ink.
That was quite a story, wasn't it,

The fur-bound book that devoured everything
And there, right there, in the book, see
R. M. Ryan, where he is writing this.

An Out-of-Town Show

It is 1955.
I am eight

riding in the back
of my Daddy's '52 Ford.

Hank Williams
on the box.

"Your Cheatin' Heart"—
and my Daddy sings along.

I look out
at the scenery passing by.

Corn fields, used-car lots,
scrap-metal yards.

What do I know?
My Daddy's never sung

before, except for the time
he hummed

"The Old Rugged Cross"
when he insisted

that he and I see *The Robe*.
The moment passes.

Hank Williams
is gone to wherever

it is he's gone to
(as happens

I later learn,
he died in the backseat

of a Cadillac convertible
on the way to

an out-of-town show).
"Another day so beautiful

it must belong to God,"
Daddy says from the front seat.

I want to ride
my new AMF Road Master

and only half-listen
to what my Father

is telling me.
My mother's favorite song

was "The Tennessee Waltz."
You could, I suppose,

put these songs
together—

"Your cheatin' heart
will tell on you"

with "My friend
stole my sweetheart from me."

You could come up
with all kinds of things,

including the reason
why I stayed in the basement

for years. Yes, you certainly could,
but I don't know anything more

than what I've told you.
Except that Daddy had a girlfriend

in a faraway town.
Oh, and that Mother was

mad because
he didn't make more money.

The scenery is still passing.
Corn fields, used-car lots,

scrap-metal yards.
My bike waits for me at home.

It is still 1955.

Figureheads

I was depressed back then
and would stare for hours
at the world,
which lay there
as if everything had died.

For some reason
I couldn't take my eyes off
Pablo Neruda's collection
of ship figureheads and wondered why
he ever bothered to get so many,

especially when the fascists
chased him out of his home on Isla Negra,
leaving the half-naked women there
to fend for themselves.
Sad, I thought, how like the times

as they scored yet another
inequity in a world where
you couldn't add up all wrongs
and yet—and yet—
Pablo Neruda seems to get

more famous each year
while the fascists, who were probably
the ones who broke his spirit and then his heart,
are mostly dust at the yearly party on Isla Negra
where everyone circles the bonfire, singing,

and the golden-painted figureheads watch,
foam in their crotches
salt spray on their tits
eyes clear, looking straight ahead,
no doubts about where they're going.

The Divine Comedy Test

for my cancer

1.
How might the poet
have improved these lines?

Say in 100 words or less
what the poet meant

by abandon all hope
ye who enter here.

Oh, don't worry, no:
you're not ever going

to be close, near
enough to death

to smell his breath
stinking over you.

Or are you?
Or will you be

that well-wisher
in his starched shirt

at the end
of a long business day,

who stands
certain that he's just come

out of duty—
"He doesn't look

the way he used to do."
That's me

he's talking about
lying there

in that bed of death,
though the pronouns

get confusing
when you or he

is close to death.
"Tsk, tsk, no,"

the visitor says,
and he—or maybe you—

looks
a little frightened

doesn't he?
as he withdraws

from the stunning light
you see ahead.

2.
I am not
with you anymore.

I've gone
to the shore of death—

the black and turgid
river: fetid, lumpy, fecal;

the black going gray
as even death

must come here at last
to die.

They say in the depths
of space you cannot

see the black without
some light,

but here the only light
is on the other shore

and the light dies
by the river side.

"Exact change only"
is what Charon says,

his moss-covered
wooden ferry boat

thumping against the piling,
the oars dripping.

He holds them high
waiting for you to pay

as you stand on the
heavy pier.

You only have
a twenty.

"Next time,"
he says in his perfect pitch.

In his perfect smile,
in his perfect teeth,

in his perfect
lichen-covered

suit he smiles
and rows away,

a hulked shadow
his only passenger

"Hurry up," the Shadow
says. "Oh, hurry. Please hurry"

as into the staggering
light they go

and you head back up
the cobwebbed steps,

the yellow-orange
imperfect light

of ordinary life
up ahead. Ah,

a coffee shop.
A small latte,

you think,
to break the twenty

and there, ah,
a cheese danish.

"Warm that up?"
"Why of course"—

the warm delight,
and all the voices

of all that's light
and lovely and living

in the world right here
in front of you,

on the altar of
the ordinary earth,

and yes I could be
Lazarus

back from the dead
or someone

who plays Lazarus
on television,

lucky to have
escaped the forest

where the dark
yews that made

my chemo poison
grow—I am coming

free into that meadow
kissing the very

air
of where I live.

The Fireworks

Tonight,
here in America,

the fireworks
are too close for comfort.

They rattle the windows
and blow apart

empty spaces
in the air,

coming
closer and closer,

as if someone
is triangulating

targets
to get to you

and me.
Gulp.

I am for the moment
terrified,

turning off the lights
the way they told us to

in the Army.
Help.

I don't know where
to run.

I think
of my brothers and sisters

in Gaza, where the tanks
are rolling tonight.

I think of long ago
battles in Vietnam,

in Iraq, in Verdun.
in wars fought, really,

simply to have a war
where they bayonet

the babies
and accomplish

nothing
but make the war go on.

"When will
they ever learn?"

goes the song.
I sob

for the idiocy
of it all.

When the fireworks
are done,

I walk out of my apartment,
and the doorman,

who's just back
from Afghanistan,

says,
"Be safe

out there.
Be safe."

The Initiation

I was pledging
the Alpha Omega

something fraternity.
It was college, right?

It was what we did
in 1964 before the War

took so many of us away,
and so I was sitting at 3 a.m.

in the backseat
of Pit Bull Johnson's

'57 DeSoto
with the floorboards rusted out,

holding on my lap

a bull's cock and balls
from the meat-packing plant,

its blood and viscera
running down my legs.

I was in a haze
of rusty metal and beer

as we drove to Iowa City.
Those were the days

when I Pabst Blue Ribboned
myself into oblivion

but—hey—wasn't this
what we did

in 1964, before the War
took so many of us away?

Then Pit Bull Johnson
and us pledges

were standing before
the famous Black Angel Statue

presenting our offering of us
and the bull cock and balls.

Pit Bull said our prayer
"Holy mackerel, holy shit:

Remember us and remember this."
He held the bull's cock and balls aloft

then threw them on the ground
and sped away, hoping I suppose

the blackness wouldn't catch up with us.
In the car, now driving fast, he sang

the On Wisconsin song of fight
as if to get us through that awful night.

That then was merely song
though I later learned that On Wisconsin

is what the hell-bent lieutenant yelled
as his men drove the Rebels from Cemetery Ridge

in the Battle of Chattanooga
oh so long ago.

What I remember now, though,
is how the wings of the Black Angel

wanted to take us in its shroud
before the War began.

The Owl and the Pussycat

The Owl and the Pussycat
are still at sea,
far from you
and far from me.

They crossed the ocean
full of hope
and sang
with great emotion.

Each day they sailed
they had their lunch
made of quince and cake.
No matter what their aches,

they kept on sailing
past foreign lands and seas.
They held on tight
to their little boat

as over the seas they went.
They sailed and sailed
until their quince was gone
over the sea, the sea.

The sail was tatters.
Pretty soon the boat was gone,
soon the Owl and Pussycat are gone as well
and all that remained was just memory.

The Owl and the Pussycat
are still at sea,
still far from you
and far from me.

The Traveling Exquisites

In Bernini's statue
of Apollo

chasing Daphne
through the woods,

perhaps beneath
the same

blue sky and cloud
you and I sit beneath—

her not so much
wanting to escape from him

but just wanting
the moment to go on—

the traveling exquisites
of a life led almost to ecstasy,

the orgasm
of the orgasm yet to come.

Look at the statue yourself.
She's not really escaping

just staying
one lovely breast away

from what his hand would touch,
and I think of them

finally in the tree,
him chasing her

for eternity
in the twists

and turns
of the first trunk

and then the branches
of the way the tree grows,

forever out of reach,
reaching for

and running
from each other.

The Trembling Hand

It started strong, sure of itself,
drawing lines ruler straight,

or the perfect ellipsis
of a cartoon head

but then—what?—age,
the fear of death,

the fear of running out of things to draw,
or just nameless, anxious fear—

it began to shake.
But what if

it weren't Parkinson's
or one of the thousand other maladies

that take us from the earth,
what if . . . could we just imagine

joy? . . . joy so exuberant
it sometimes took

two hands to hold it down.
Maybe God was drawing then.

Wasn't that
what Einstein said—

that he was simply
taking dictation?

Maybe it's one hand
holding on,

while the other's
shaken

with celestial song.

What I Heard

This morning on the river
Someone's hammering.

It sounds right next door,
As if I could pick the hammer up,

But it's a mile away.
Strange the way distances collapse.

"Hello," I yell.
"Hello," he answers back,

As if he's right here.
As if, as if:

I'm rattling
The doorway to eternity.

The ducks rise up, slapping the water with their wings,
As if they're applauding themselves

For the way they're rising
This morning on the river.

The Book of All There Is

Gulls. Thousands
and thousands of them

swirling here,
where the river

comes into the ocean.
They circle around me

and I turn
then turn again—

a dance
in the center

of something.
The gulls

and all that white flutter
like pages torn

from an important book.
The Book of All There Is

perhaps—whirling around me.
If only I could touch them,

I might read. . . .
But then, the gulls

aren't pages in a book,
and I am only me,

standing there,
and it all

gets
away from me

as I try
and try again

to say
what I cannot say,

getting nowhere
faster than I meant,

standing here
dizzy

and out of breath
circled by thousands

and thousands of gulls,
standing here,

with nothing
but a handful of sky.

The Sparrow

I wonder, was he playing hide and seek
With me this morning, 5 a.m., inside
My house, from the ficus plant to the Christmas tree,

Flying from the living to the dining room,
Me chasing him back and forth, out
Of breath, trying to talk him into leaving.

"Aren't you cute?" Then he-she—how
Do you tell the sex of a sparrow?—
Just beyond the towel I held, me

Not quick enough. This had gone on for an hour,
Me noticing suddenly how beautiful
A sparrow is, no wonder God sees

Their every move—the white band around
Their eyes, the alternating tan and white
Feathers interlaced across their chests

Like fingers of some hidden hand, protecting
Them, then whoops, I'm down, 6 a.m.,
These damn slippers tripping me up, the sparrow

Fluttering just overhead, how vivid his eyes are,
I notice, him watching me, his vivid eyes,
His eyes, yes, his eyes watching my every move.

The Confessions of the Professor

I admit
I wanted to reach
inside her curves.

Just
a touch
and nothing more—

run the lightest
finger
along

the feathered
feelings
of her thighs.

That's all.
Oh, I gave her books—
The Rainbow, Lycidas

with those lists
of flowers
we have to penetrate

if we're to live
in what is real
instead of what

we pretend
is real.
She's gone,

the girl is,
muddied
by my touch

as if
she'd laid down
in dirt

for me
to mount her
as I'm doing here,

framing her
in a story
of my own

while she's
out there
herself somewhere

with my books
and a story
of her own

that I hope
begins
You wouldn't

believe
what the old rascal
did to me.

PART V

Art Is Long, Life Is Short, and All the Rest of It

I heard somewhere of an artist who stood before
a firing squad and begged, "Please don't shoot me.
My drawings are beautiful." The Captain of the Guard

was bored, having shot so many in the sun that day.
"Let's see," he said and ordered pen and paper
brought in. The artist drew furiously and got the scene:

the wall smudged with blood, the squad of men
in their rumpled uniforms, some leaning on the rifles,
others smoking, the dead man stretched out,

the litter bearers just arriving, the mountains
and the sun above the rest of it. "Pretty good,"
the Captain said, but shot him anyway,

and the artist fell, thinking as he died,
the pen isn't mightier than much of anything,
though his fall completed what his drawing showed,

or did when the litter bearers got there,
and the Captain moved into the shadowed foreground.
He held the drawing up, trying to figure out

how the scene varied from the way the afternoon
had gone, the afternoon so quickly done,
the afternoon now fading in the sun.

This Morning

It's 7 a.m.
The boy slowly walks,
his heavy backpack

bends him down
like a porter
for a mountain-climbing party.

It's probably full
of algebra and poetry.
How old is he—15? 16?

The heavy world
of knowledge
on his back.

Going to school,
where his teacher
will ask him to solve

the unsolvable mystery of X
or what Keats meant
by "easeful death."

And he will write
with the dusty chalk
made from the ashes of creatures

a million years dead
on the blackboard
of Caesar and Thermopylae

unintentionally
what the ashes
really mean.

O heavy
is the darkening world
that will try to crush him

the first day
he is late for work
or the month

the stock market
collapses or when
he trips

and blood forms
around his head
like a black halo.

Thank God
for the small bird—
a grackle perhaps—

running along the sidewalk
as if
to catch up with him,

a yellow rose petal
in its beak
maybe to let him know

that the world
is filled with beauty
even in what falls away

and that the smallest bird—
black, insignificant—
has a chance to fly.

Beethoven

You could see him
hurrying by
on the Herrengasse,

The street of The Lords—
of God, really, before
The Lords

got hold of it,
hurrying, his head bowed,
as if the gods

were all round him,
his hands clasped before him
perhaps in prayer.

In der Eile
he writes his friends,
always in a hurry

to get it down,
like Keats
trying to get his soul

on paper,
so the Herrengasse
might find its own.

Growing deaf
to the world
and its enticing nonsense.

He puts his one
good ear to the floor
to hear his student's

piano notes
echo through
the apartment building,

the music of the spheres
crashing through his head,
God's music overwhelming him.

He can hardly walk
on the Herrengasse,
Die Tochter aus Elysium

calling him, this broken man,
for the march
to the heights ahead.

The D minor chords,
Schiller's words
Alle menschen werden Brüder

on the Herrengasse.
The people back away
from this crazy impoverished man

humming, shaking his head
as if to lose a curse.
The people stare

and throw him pfennigs
and he stares back,
at something only he can see,

humming a tune only he can hear.

Backyard Salvation

My God,
you talk about

your miracles—
here is the hummingbird,

its fierce hovering
in the salvia,

in the *salvia*
for Christ's sake,

as if
she would be saved

drinking
the sweet nectar,

this delicate juice,
"the drink of the gods."

There's so little of it
to go around—

salvation here
in the backyard—

and her head turns
suddenly, and there's a

fluorescent
purple flare

along her neck,
and she turns again.

Now her head's a dull black,
a trick of the sunlight perhaps

taking us from
beautiful to dull

and back again.
Perhaps her body

fiercely resists itself
when it flowers into the purple

irradiance of
the salvia.

An Ecstatic Everywhere

I went to sleep
and shivered

with ecstasy—
the kind

that shakes
your whole body.

What was that
about?

I was listening
to Chopin

before I fell asleep.
One of the Ballades.

Which one?
Then Steve,

the bee guy, came over,
"Had a feeling

something
was going on."

We took
the roof

off the hive,
and the bees

were shivering
with their own kind

of ecstasy.
The Queen

was singing.
"Oh my," Steve said,

"I have only heard
that once before in my life."

What is it
about this world

that keeps
sending

us messages?
Later that day

I picked up a book
on the bookstore sale table

and read
somewhere in middle:

"The sunlight
poured through the front door."

I read this
over and over

as I stood there
in the sunlight.

Just Now

Beneath the huge
expanse of sky

the sparrow
and I

met
where he waited

beside a single
purple petal

along our common way.
He looked at me

and then he nodded
at the flower

and flew away
as if this tiny petal

was meant
just for me.

I'd Be a Rainbow If I Could

So there I was
standing beside

this homeless guy
as the rainbow

moved toward us,
a blessing of everyday.

He told me
"I'm Jimmy Dean."

He actually
kind of looked

like Jimmy Dean.
"The song 'Honeycomb,'

right?" I asked.
"On second thought,

I'm Elvis.
I never thought

he was really dead.
He sold more records

after he was supposedly dead
than when he was alive."

"Cool," I said.
That's what everyone says

when they don't know what to say.
"That's me," he said.

"Cool as a Kelvinator."
We stood there together

smoking,
our little fires

turning into ash.
"Look at that," he said,

pointing at
the bent-over stop sign.

"Couldn't stand up
to the world—

Me, I'm still upright."
"Me, too," I said,

and we laughed at that,
two guys against the world

beneath the rainbow
disappearing

as it moved
over us.

"You know what?"
he asked.

"I'd be a rainbow
if I could.

A speck there in the blue,
shining in the sun."

"Me, too," I said.
"Me, too."

The Pleiades, the Pleiades

Maybe this is Mozart,
and we're just
in another part of the forest

instead of where
the real action is.
Look: I'll sing

"*Der Vogelfänger bin ich ja,*"
and you say "*Stille, stille, stille,*"
and everything will be just fine.

Oh no.
Hear that?
It's that damn

Wasteland Sing-Along.
They just take over
the whole town,

with those bass singers
who think they're so, so *profoundo*—
and the sopranos! with their descants

dancing across the tragedies
as if the other guy's bad news
were just a stage for them.

Too bad.
The Pleiades aren't going to help you out of this
but it's fun to say

The Pleiades, The Pleiades
over and over. It's a kind of chorus
to the unforgettable song

we'll write next week.
You'll be der Vogelfänger then,
and I'll say *"Stille, stille, stille"*

as we wander through the National Forest,
trying to count the trees,
someone dancing and singing overhead—

The Pleiades, The Pleiades.

The War

It was the summer of 1969,
just about the time
America landed on the moon.

I was in Louisiana then—
Fifth Platoon of Company B,
Third Basic Training Brigade.

"First in the Field" was our motto.
In fact there were mottos everywhere.
"Follow Me"—the cry of infantry

was right over the drinking fountain.
There was also The Code of the Bayonet,
which was the word "Kill"

repeated over and over
in the stunning sunshine
of Fort Polk, Louisiana,

training us to be killers,
Charpentier, Lewis, and me,
our M-14's held close to our chests

for an exercise called Range Fire.
A few of us ran down lanes
with a drill sergeant behind

each of us yelling "Kill,
you motherfucker" and pounding
on our steel helmets with their clipboards.

The targets popped up
in that stunning sunshine
and we dropped to our knees

like men approaching the altar
and tried to hit the target.
"Stop" someone screamed.

"Stop" and we all stood up
and looked around the way
we always did—like dogs

when their choke collar's pulled
and sure enough Lewis
had mistakenly shot Charpentier

and the air filled with helicopters
and the ground with generals
and then one by one they all left,

the last one standing on the step
of the helicopter squinting
into the stunning sunshine

as if he was in a movie.
"So long, boys," he said,
waving at us. "We got us

a war to win," With that
he rose up into the heavens
leaving behind the sound

of his helicopter
walloping the air.

The Landfill We Protected So Carefully

I don't know about you
but I am more than just a little worried
about civilization.

I keep imagining
a Harrison Ford kind of guy
in his epaulet-shouldered khakis

and pith helmet with his shovel
digging up that landfill just outside of town
and finding buried plastic bags,

some filled with leaves, some filled
with dog poop and cat litter.
This is, of course, the landfill

we protected so carefully:
no water, no air:
where we've perfectly preserved

T-bones from 1972
and cans of Classic Coke.
The town of course

is gone by now
these thousands of years
after us. Gone as well

is the little bistro
near the Eiffel Tower
where we fell in love

over mussels
and a chilled bottle
of Chablis.

The Eiffel Tower
is iron oxide in the Pacific;
the Picasso Museum

small pieces
of color that look
like something torn

from the funny papers
stuck to the walls
of a canyon in Idaho.

The Pyramids are Nebraska dust
the Great Wall a line
in the sand, the Tower

of London a tale
told by a homeless
idiot at a country inn

that glows in the night
like a radium watch dial.
Most of what you treasure

is gone.
There are just these bags
of leaves and poop

perfectly preserved,
and the epaulet-shouldered
Harrison Ford in his pith helmet

has—what else?—a clipboard
that has somehow survived
fires, wars, and plagues.

He begins a new page.
"The Leaf- and Poop-Saving People
disappeared. We don't know why,"

he writes with authority.
I see this all too clearly
as I walk Duvall Street

in Key West, Florida,
where everyone seems
happy to be alive.

Good for them, I think,
as I toss my paper cup
into the street trash bin,

where a name tag
has been stuck.
Your heart is now at rest

it says as the sun
suddenly comes from behind
a cloud briefly blanching

all of us to shadows.
"I love you all," I say,
though no one's really listening

as we walk along
more or less together, close enough
to hold each other's hands

as we head on home
a word, which, for another brief moment,
sounds like Om.

"*Om, Shanti, Om,*" I say
as we head for home,
my heart filled with love.

The Mystery

The time will come, Stranger,
when you won't know who you are.

The dolphins you saw that day at sea
rising to the sunshine and the sky

sang a chorus just for you.
The ruins in the desert

aligned precisely with the pathways
of the sun and moon

soon laid out the road
you are traveling now.

The writings on the temple walls
half-obliterated

by those who stood for war
and chains instead of ecstasy

will someday take you to
the algebra you have to solve

in the dreams where you meet
people you've never seen before.

And when, Stranger,
you lie ecstatic

with your lover in your bed
and cry, "My God, my God,"

your soul a rainbow now will rise
to shimmer in the sunshine and the sky.

Let's Take the Grand View

Why shouldn't this road
outside of Verona, Wisconsin,

be called Epic Lane?
Poems start

from everywhere.
Odysseus

setting out from Troy—
you setting out

from anywhere.
You could be

Stephen Daedalus
trying to get laid—

or, for instance,
Nick Englebert.

"Grandview"
is the sculpture garden

he built by hand
on his farm outside of

Hollandale, right there
on Highway 39:

Snow White made
of rocky concrete,

sea shells
covering up

her breasts.
Paul Bunyan

used to be
beside her.

Now it's just
his cement shoes—

now it's nothing,
but Nick himself made his stand

against the terrible
interrogations of time.

A thousand
million years from now

someone
will wonder

what these two
seashells are doing

on Highway 39
far from the sea.

Perhaps in Odysseus'
untold story

he took seashells
along for luck.

The concrete
Hurdy Gurdy man

stands guard
at "Grandview."

His little monkey
is waiting still

(though Nick's
been dead for years).

"Thank you, Mister,"
his little sign reads.

Thank you, indeed,
to those who

pause for stories
just to see,

what happens
when Odysseus sets out to sea.

Why the Wild Animals Stay Away from You

Quaint, huh,
these totem figures.

Even the McDonalds
here in Waimanalo, Hawaii,

has one, a little
local charm,

this Lanaikila O Waimanalo—
this man's howling red face:

a warrior surely
with a living owl for a headdress,

a living shark for body armor.
Something to reckon with, eh?

The memory of a past
fierce beyond figuring,

but, then, no one
could look like that,

could they?
Of course not.

It's just
an artistic interpretation,

a little poetic license,
but what if

there was a time,
barely a memory now,

before men had
spears and guns and atomic bombs,

when people and animals
really worked together?—

an owl for vision,
the kind of wisdom

that sees far ahead—
and a shark:

the Mano he was called,
with teeth to chew

their common enemies.
Maybe *that* was

in the famous Garden
before a bunch of rabbis

and missionaries
showed up

with their accusing fingers
to explain that men

had dominion
over all the animals,

out here in East of Eden.
You know the story, don't you?

Out here in every breath
of putrid air

you take
as the wild animals,

each and every one of them,
stay far away from you.

O, the Angels, O

You have your miracles,
and I have mine.

That time, for instance, at Mt. Shasta,
when I didn't want to go

to one of those pageants
designed, mostly, to collect money

for the priests with their statues
and their sour music and their guilty verdicts

and their version of redemption
hidden behind some stone

and the way they hurry us out of here
with a little incense and myrrh

to get the rest of our money.
Ugh. Not that, no. Not the centuries

of lies and robes. No, I was looking
for a little real magic and got some that night

in the half-finished bedroom of the broken house:
Angels. You heard me. Angels.

Dreams of angels: and not your vague
blue-dome-climbing angels painted in the upper

regions of the church. Oh my, no. My angels
were vivid as vivid could be, following me

up the street to get a latte.
One was royal blue, one mint green, the last golden yellow.

They weren't in costumes, no. Every inch of their bodies
was color. Even their wings were fluorescent

against the dull gray-brown of the earth as if to mean
that life might be even more vivid than we thought.

Their wings rattled and whirred like those
of giant hummingbirds. My angels flew

close to the ground, right behind me,
a little band of four-foot-tall protectors

that were as real as you sitting there—
as real as the hundreds of golden butterflies that flickered

and then landed all over the bare skin of my body
that afternoon along the Madre de Dios River

in the Amazon. "Salt, of course, they
were after salt, but salt's a kind of miracle

in the jungle, and, well, you know, I've never heard
of an encounter like that, I mean, you covered

with golden butterflies. That's really something,"
our guide said, a kind of wonder in his face,

the kind of wonder I am feeling right now
as I think of you sitting here, reading this.

Writing My Vows

The owl—
a ghost spiral in the dark—

searches for something
moving in the night grass.

I by my study light
work on my homework.

I am writing my vows
for my Zen happiness class.

To the owl,
I must be

nothing
but a burning speck.

Even so,
I vow

to live a life
of passionate simplicity,

a calm intelligence
between the arias

of ecstasy and despair
even when I know

that the dragon
looks for me.

She lifts her head.
Perhaps she

is the only one
who hears my song.

She lifts her head,
as afraid of the dark

as I am,
ready

to devour me
as I search, a ghostly

spiral in the dark,
for the treasure

I will find
myself

a part of some day
guarded by the dragon

while the owl—
a haze of phosphorous

in the dark—
searches

& searches & searches
for the perfect thing

moving
in the night grass.

What the Guide Said

Welcome
to the dragon's cave.

Please. Have a seat.
We used to have

these fire-proof suits.
They worked just fine

but the people, alas,
baked to death inside.

So Lesson One is
You Take Your Chances

and—oh, yes—you can
Pay Your Money right here to me.

Thanks.
I've forgotten

what Lesson Two is.
Oh well.

I'd give you a tour
but eventually

you'll have to go
all by yourself

so you might as well
get started.

I hope your rituals
help, whatever they might be.

You can do quadratic equations
or wear a robe and sing Hallelujah.

Use syllogisms to rule things out.
Burn incense. Whatever.

You'll be good to go.
But the brightness in that dark

is not, I'm afraid,
like anything you've seen before

—or will likely see again.
Let's just hope

there's a treasure
on the other side.

The Song Sparrow

Consider,
please,

the song
sparrow,

half-heard,
this little bundle

of energy
tossing

up dirt
and turning

this way
and that,

turning around
again,

starting
over,

as if he's looking
for something in the dirt.

Singing
for all he's worth.

All this song
must mean something,

coming out of this little
Buddha of Joy,

two inches
of Beethoven's Fifth,

and I think
of Leonard Bernstein—

who'd be dead
in a couple of months—

someone helping him to the podium,
not enough

strength, leaning there,
to lift Beethoven

out of the earth,
conducting with his eyes

the Fifth Symphony,
the twirling and chirp

of an entire orchestra,
the audience

bent over
in their seats

as if praying
for us all to sing.

Nothing Goes Away

Oh, look,
my pockets

are full of sand.
I wonder

where it came from.
Somewhere else,

that's for sure.
Maybe once

it was part
of a towering city

now in ruins—
or gone,

the way Atlantis is.
My dog sniffs

the currents
of the ocean air

that came
from somewhere else as well,

as did the oil
that fuels

our furious
back and forth—

vast jungles
of palms and ferns

laid slowly
down

to rot
into this golden

energy.
The dog

could be sniffing
Leonardo's breath

as he hurried
across the Piazza del Duomo.

Nothing goes away.
It circles

the earth
as if looking for a home.

Even the lowly
fly caught

with sunlight behind
has an amber

abdomen
that glows

like a jewel.
The sands

run through my fingers
like someone else's hours

now my own
as I breathe in

the breath of sailors
looking for their home.

This Lovely Dalliance

It surely looks like love,
these two geckos embracing.

Me watching from above
as the afternoon is fleeing.

He's bigger, with an orange stripe.
She lies beneath him,

a dusky blue radiance.
He's thrusting. Yipes.

It looks a lot more like us
than I ever would have discussed.

He occasionally leans toward her head,
and she looks back at him,

both now undulating together up and down,
blind to what anyone has said.

Tender the way her radiance
fades and glows in this lovely dalliance.

Afterwards he puffs his bright orange bladder out,
and she lies there trembling like the evening sky.

So exquisite this moment is.
How lucky I was to see it there,

this tingle in the midst of time,
in this world where we all must die.

Me and the Woman with a Statue of a Dog

Headed north this morning,
A woman with a statue of a dog

In a basket with a bouquet of artificial flowers.
Me writing here

On how I used to drink:
It was just so glamorous

The names of all those wines—
Cabernet, Pinot Grigio, Côtes du Rhône—

Expertly pronounced,
Rolling off my working-class tongue

To prove just how far I'd come
From the night shift at Fairbanks Morse.

I got high all right—
Not quite to the top

But to the 29th floor
Of the US Bank building,

Holding forth at $300 an hour.
"A better class of illusion"

Is what my old boss said.
Peter's dead

And so, too, is the meaning of that money
Here now in the last years of my life.

I gave up the wine—couldn't stand the black
Willies of 3 a.m., so I, too, travel north

Clear-headed, the sky smeared
With wild-fire smoke.

It's hard to breathe
But I'm going to smile

As I keep walking to join the dead.
What else is there to do, really,

But sing my off-key tune?
Perhaps I should go arm-in-arm

With the woman carrying the statue of a dog
As if it might make a difference,

Me and the woman with the statue of a dog,
Arm and arm, walking up the road.

The Rosebud

I have—
petal

by exquisite
petal,

the anthology
of pinks

of yellows—
tried

to put
the rosebud

back together
again.

The wind
eventually

takes
them.

Perhaps,
somewhere,

the fallen
angels

fly
once more.

The Inflated Santa on My Neighbor's Roof

He rises with the 20-degree wind,
Like a man taking a deep breath,

Then bends flat with the day
As if all those gifts

Have worn him down.
His head tips back. He's laughing.

His head falls forward with exhaustion
Then rises up as if he's just remembered

The electric train you wanted,
The dolls you never got—

He has them wrapped for you at last
Courtesy of the wind, the turning of the earth,

The miracle of gifts, the miracle of being
Empty-handed, catching nothing

But his death of cold. He slumps.
An old man now,

I rock back and forth
From over here at your neighbor's house.

See: I'm rising now with this, my gift to you,
Slumping with this, this other gift,

Empty handed, I give you what I have,
Gift wrapped, this. This. This.

Workingman's Dead: The Poetry of Ray Carver

"And Death shall have no dominion."
Big talk, baby—and certainly memorable,
But the no dominion part? That happens after we're dead.
On the way to the rotting dock when Charon waits
it's a nail biter, baby. Enough to drive a sane man mad.
Or to drink or drugs or cigarettes or all the above.

"Half in love with easeful death" John Boy Keats said,
attracted to what he feared the most.
And he succeeded, didn't he? Done by 25.
Our-Death-shall-have-no-dominion lad?—
why Dylan Thomas was gone by 39.
To be or not to be is the real question

on the major-field examination
when you get into the English and American
literature game. Our man today,
the redoubtable Ray Carver, was finished at 50.
Is there something in the literary water?
Ray was headed for the Other Side

from the very start. It's in the first poem
in the *Collected Poems*—"I would gladly," he writes
"lie down and sleep forever." Death is there
so often in all these poems you'll lose count
trying to tally up the Dark Guy's presence.
But isn't this what the workers on the assembly line,

the ones just up ahead breaking stones in the mine,
even the ones showing up to teach boneheads
how to write: isn't this what the workers want?
The glamorous first class ticket to the Other Side,
the black Cadillac one-way limo ride to the memorial park,
the 4 by 8 foot testimonial named just for you, baby.

The workingman's day off is getting sick.
Her sabbatical is a round of chemo.
Retirement is a wooden box.
"Will you miss me when I'm gone?"
A. P. Carter's lament in that country song goes.
By dying I show you how important I was.

By dying I put all my cards on the table.
and hope I'll win on The Other Side.
This is the way to go, isn't it,
even though the mourners don't care much for your music:
the stately iambs, the turn, the counter turn
and stand of English and American poetry

It's Hallelujah on the way, the common sidewalk
now a promenade, the ecstatic walk of Death.
You bet we love this stuff, knowing that underneath
the sex and the cigarettes we're walking down
what Philip Larkin called the cemetery road,
especially now, in the Iron Age of Anxiety

we're mostly done with miracles, the only miracle left
is the Long Goodbye of our exit from the stage.
So when a poet nails it, really gets us
on the cross, we rise to the occasion
our own little Empyrean among the nouns and verbs,
the surprise of our off-key Hallelujah breaking from our throats.

The Rubaiyat, Etc.

The moving finger,
having writ, moves on.

He's just a finger
with a frown

who's off to another gig
in yet another town.

What he's written—
how easy to forget,

so he's simplified his song
to just this tune:

The sun comes up, the sun goes down.
The big old world goes spinning round.

We're the chorus.
Why don't you sing along?

EPILOGUE

From My Backyard

in memory of Tom Garst

1.

Sure there's Beethoven—
but we have joys of our own.
Let's get the Tochter aus Elysium

out of here—or least turn
the volume down.
There.

It's been much better
since I gave my high school
memories a C and that

mostly for trying.
All those bad ideas in a style
stiff as a sophomore speech.

I mean, you know,
I liked the beat,
but the words weren't much.

You could dance to it—
but who gets this joke anymore?
Besides, it really isn't

exactly funny
when I've become
older than I ever could have imagined

when I turned my crotch this way and that
at those CYO dances in 1962.
Maybe that's why I keep

walking East Memorial Drive
for the answers to the questions
I have trouble asking

and why I failed all the tests
of the Emergency Broadcast System.
Here, for instance, is Mrs. Clark's

basement window where I put
the cinders out every Sunday evening
in 1962 and was bitter because I was

putting cinders out for fifty cents a week
while the rest of the world
stayed home watching *Maverick* on TV.

Here I am three years later,
home from college going north
in my backyard with the lawn mower

along the garage and past
the sandbox then west
beside the raspberries

that grab at me as if
they don't want me to go on.
I turn south by the grape arbor

and go past the peonies and the crabapple tree
that bloom splendidly every other year,
then east along the house

and the pear trees that in other years
were all the bases in the baseball games
I played by myself.

It was someone's
idea of Eden,
I realize now as I write

this out, but then—
oh then I worked
in ever smaller circles (the mower

against the garden)
to the place my father sits,
smoking, in a lawn chair,

its webbing like plaid across his back
or maybe like a crossword puzzle.
When it was over,

we found Carter's Little Liver Pills
in his dresser. He kept saying
"I never thought it was in my lungs"

and I—
I never thought
I'd come back here for this.

2.
Let's see.
Our original topic
was joy—and its existence here.

The great quotes are in German
natürlich, but life has a way
of going on around the statues

in the *allée*, which have,
if you look closely,
begun to decay.

In the spring of 1965,
the spring of the year
my father died of lung cancer,

I started out for Selma, Alabama,
to save the world, though I myself
was too chicken to call

my parents and ask their permission.
"Tell them," my roommate said,
"it's like a field trip

only a little farther away
and, of course, longer and just a bit
more dangerous."

We had a pastor leading us
and the only jock at my college
interested in civil rights

driving a rusty '59 Ford
when we set off to take the Truth
we had in Iowa south. I kept calling

home from pay phones along the road,
but the line was busy.
We rear-ended a car,

and I remember
that the man in the car we hit
was an insurance agent who had

a Speed Graphic in his trunk.
He photographed the cars and the scenery
and us as we stood

around talking and staring
at him. "You can never tell,"
he said, "when you'll need a camera

to record the truth."
Four hours after starting out
I was barely twenty miles away

when I finally talked to my uncle.
He told me to come home.
"Your father is dying of cancer,"

he said. "You don't have time
for civil rights."
It was my roommate who ended up

ten feet down from Joan Baez
in the famous photograph
of the Good while I—

I stayed out of History
to watch my father die.
That summer, I worked

at the Chevrolet assembly plant
where they locked us in like prisoners
at 7 a.m. and let us out when the whistle

blew at 3:30 in the afternoon.
As my father got weaker,
I had to shave him

every third day.
He seemed to drift
farther and farther inside himself,

his eyes so large in all that wasted flesh.
As I shaved him my face was only
inches away from him.

We hardly spoke.
It was embarrassing to have
a dying father when I wanted to

touch Patsy O'Conner's breasts.
I didn't know
that her father and mother both were drunks

and that she'd be one, too,
later leaving behind her husband
and her children for booze.

That summer, I tried to write but stayed
locked inside myself the way I was locked
inside that Chevrolet assembly plant.

That summer, I read Rimbaud's *Illuminations*
and underlined in the book I still have
"There is no sovereign music for our desire."

Oh Papageno, the pilgrimage
is much easier when you have
the music.

The memory of my father
that keeps coming back
is the two of us up at 4

in the morning, he because
he liked that hour and me
because I had to fold and deliver

The Rockford Morning Star.
I remember sitting by the backstairs,
my hands squeaky dry

with newsprint as if the news
were dark and rubbed off
on everything and smelled

vaguely like fish.
"He's Got the Whole World in His Hands"
played on the radio

while I worked and my father
smoked and drank coffee
and then we were off

into the dark morning,
me on my AMF Roadmaster
with a steel basket

to deliver the news to Janesville,
he to the job that gave him
a nervous breakdown.

I read today that a cybernetic
picture of *pi* looks like
the Himalayas and that the billion

or more numbers they've found
behind the decimal point
would stretch from New York

to Kansas and beyond to infinity
as if the mathematics of the circling world
eventually become infinity itself.

Back then, in 1962, I didn't know
any of this, didn't know that I have only
three more years to argue

with my father.
Back then, I was walking
home from Mrs. Clark's,

my hands covered with cinder ashes
under a limitless expanse of stars.
Back then, I'm a block away

from The Cozy Corner
where Cokes cost a nickel
and six Elvis tunes on the Wurlizter

cost a quarter.
I have fifty cents in my pocket.
The money belongs to me

and to me alone.
My chores are done,
and the smell of supper's in the air.